Contents

INTRODUCTION

Network Topology is a structural network layout that is either physical or logical and arranged by a pattern of connected computers, devices, nodes, and other links of a network. It has different structures of a network topology that shows how a network is created and connected a link (in different methods) to a device. Such network topology structures are bus, ring, mesh, fully connected (or complete), star, and hierarchical (tree). Computers MUST connect to a network of any topology because of information sharing and communication. Without a network, users are unable to share files, send emails, print files, creating and sharing database, etc. An example of this is a Local Area Network (LAN). Any node in the LAN has one or more links to other devices within the network, mapping these links can result in a geometric shape.

NETWORK TOPOLOGY

Network Topology refers to the layout of a network and how different nodes in a network are connected to each other and how they communicate. Topologies are either physical (the physical layout of devices on a network) or logical (the way that the signals act on the network media, or the way that the data passes through the network from one device to the next). This Webopedia Study Guide describes five of the most common network topologies.

A network topology is the arrangement of nodes -- usually switches, routers, or software switch/router features -- and connections in a network, often represented as a graph. The topology of the network, and the relative locations of the source and destination of traffic flows on the network, determine the optimum path for each flow and the extent to which redundant options for routing exist in the event of a failure. There are two ways of defining network geometry: the physical topology and the logical (or signal) topology.

Physical Topology

The physical topology of a network is the layout of nodes and physical connections, including wires (Ethernet, DSL), fiber optics, and microwave. There are several common physical topologies, as described below and as shown in the illustration.

Types of Physical Topologies

In the bus network topology, every node is connected in series along a linear path. This arrangement is found today primarily in cable broadband distribution networks.

In the star network topology, a central node has a direct connection to all other nodes. Switched local-area networks (LANs) based on Ethernet switches, including most wired home and office networks, have a physical star topology.

In the ring network topology, the nodes are connected in a closed loop configuration. Some rings will pass data only in one direction, while others are capable of transmission in both directions. These bidirectional ring networks are more resilient than bus networks because traffic can reach a node by moving in either direction. Metro networks based on Synchronous Optical Network Technology (SONET) are the primary example of ring networks today.

The mesh network topology links nodes with connections so that multiple paths between at least some points of the network are available. A network is said to be fully meshed if all nodes are directly connected to all other nodes, and partially meshed if only some nodes have multiple connections to others. Meshing to create multiple paths increases resiliency under failure, but increases cost. The Internet is a mesh network.

The tree network topology, also called a star of stars, is a network where star topologies are themselves connected in a star configuration. Many larger Ethernet switch networks including data center networks, are configured as trees.

Logical Topologies

A logical topology for a network usually refers to the relationship between nodes and logical connections. A logical connection will differ from a physical path when information can take an invisible hop at intermediate points. In optical networks, optical add-drop multiplexers (ADMs) create logical optical paths because the ADM hop isn't visible to the endpoint nodes. Networks based on virtual circuits (or tunnels) will have a physical topology based on the real connection medium (fiber, for example) and a logical topology based on the circuits/tunnels.

Sometimes the logical topology will refer to the topology as the user sees it, which means the connectivity of the network. IP and Ethernet networks, the two most commonly used today, are fully meshed at the connection level because any user can connect with any other -- unless some means of blocking unwanted connections, like a firewall, is introduced. This full connectivity is a property of the network protocols used (IP and Ethernet), not of the network topology itself. Any network topology can appear to be fully meshed to its users.

Types of Network Topology

The arrangement of a network which comprises of nodes and connecting lines via sender and receiver is referred as network topology. The various network topologies are :

The Mesh Topology

In the mesh topology each computer is connected to each of the other computers. If you have six computers you would need five network cards in each computer to connect to all the other computers in the LAN. This topology is very expensive as you need a cable run to all the other computers in the building and a network connection for each. To add computers to the network you would have to add a cable run and a network card to each computer. This topology (Figure 1.12) requires the most cable and hardware to keep the network running. On the plus side, at least if links or computers go down there are always multiple paths to get the data through. The Internet is considered a partial mesh topology as there are multiple paths through the backbone.

There are two techniques to transmit data over the Mesh topology, they are :

1. Routing
2. Flooding

Mesh Topology: Routing

In routing, the nodes have a routing logic, as per the network requirements. Like routing logic to direct the data to reach the destination using the shortest distance. Or, routing logic which has information about the broken links, and it avoids those node etc. We can even have routing logic, to re-configure the failed nodes.

Mesh Topology: Flooding

In flooding, the same data is transmitted to all the network nodes, hence no routing logic is required. The network is robust, and the its very unlikely to lose the data. But it leads to unwanted load over the network.

A mesh topology has multiple connections, making it the most fault tolerant topology available. Every component of the network is connected directly to every other component. Characteristics of a mesh topology are as follows:

- A mesh topology provides redundant links across the network.
  If a break occurs in a segment of cable, traffic can still be rerouted using the other cables.
- This topology is rarely used because of the significant cost and work involved in having network components directly connected to every other component.
- It is common for partial mesh topologies to be deployed. This balances cost and the need for redundancy.

Features of Mesh Topology

1. It transmits data only in one direction.
2. Every device is connected to a single cable

In mesh topology, every device is connected to another device via particular channel.

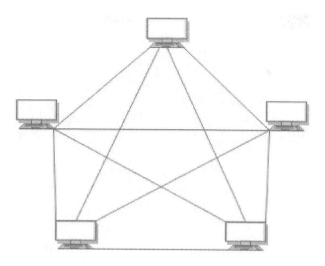

Figure 1 : Every device is connected with another via dedicated channels. These channels are known as links.

- If suppose, N number of devices are connected with each other in mesh topology, then total number of ports that is required by each device is N-1. In the Figure 1, there are 5 devices connected to each other, hence total number of ports required is 4.

- If suppose, N number of devices are connected with each other in mesh topology, then total number of dedicated links required to connect them is $^NC_2$ i.e. N(N-1)/2. In the Figure 1, there are 5 devices connected to each other, hence total number of links required is 5*4/2 = 10.

Advantages of this topology :

- It is robust.
- Fault is diagnosed easily. Data is reliable because data is transferred among the devices through dedicated channels or links.
- Provides security and privacy.

Problems with this topology :

- Installation and configuration is difficult.
- Cost of cables are high as bulk wiring is required, hence suitable for less number of devices.
- Cost of maintenance is high.

Star Topology

A star topology is a network topology in which all the network nodes are individually connected to a central switch, hub or computer which acts as a central point of communication to pass on the messages.

In a star topology, there are different nodes called hosts and there is a central point of communication called server or hub. Each host or computer is individually connected to the central hub. We can also term the server as the root and peripheral hosts as the leaves.

In this topology, if nodes want to communicate with a central node, then they pass on the message to the central server and the central server forwards their messages to the different nodes. Thus, they form a topology like the representation of a star.

How does Communication Happen in a Star Topology?

Let's say all the computers of a floor are connected to a common hub or switch. The switch maintains a CAM table in this case. The CAM table is Content Addressable Memory where hardware addresses of the all the connected devices are stored inside a memory in the switch.

For example, if computer A wants to send a data packet to computer B then computer A will forward the message to the switch. The switch will check the address of the destination computer and forward the message to the same.

In the case of a hub, a hub has no memory of its own. So when computer A sends a message to computer B, then hub announces "Hello all the ports connected to me, I have got a packet for this address. Who of you has this address?" This procedure is called

ARP (Address Resolution Protocol) and using this network protocol the hub is able to find the address of the intended machine and hence, it transfers the packet to the destination machine.

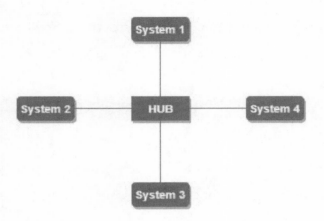

Figure 2 : A star topology having four systems connected to single point of connection i.e. hub.

Advantages of this topology :

- If N devices are connected to each other in star topology, then the number of cables required to connect them is N. So, it is easy to set up.
- Each device require only 1 port i.e. to connect to the hub.

Problems with this topology :

- If the concentrator (hub) on which the whole topology relies fails, the whole system will crash down.
- Cost of installation is high.
- Performance is based on the single concentrator i.e. hub.

Bus Topology

Alternatively referred to as a line topology, a bus topology is a network setup where each computer and network device is connected to a single cable or backbone. Depending on the type of computer network card, a coaxial cable or an RJ-45 network cable is used to connect them together. A bus topology consists of a single cable with the terminator at each end. All present nodes are connected to the single cable. There is no limit to the no: of nodes that can be attached to this network, but the no: of connected nodes can actually affect the performance of the network.

In a bus topology, one of the nodes acts as the server and transmits the data from one end to the other in a single direction. When the data reaches the extreme end, the terminator removes the data from the line.

In a bus topology, one main cable acts as the backbone for the entire network. The bus topology carries the transmitted data along the cable. As the data reaches each node, the node checks the destination address (MAC/IP address) to see if it matches their address. If the address doesn't match, the node does nothing more. But if the node addresses match to the address contained in the data then they process on the information.

The Backbone cable in the bus topology depends on the type of network card used in each computer, an RJ-45 network cable or coaxial cable is used to connect them together.

Features of Bus topology

A bus topology basically consists of devices connected through a single cable which is shared among all the connected devices. It is many a times called as "linear bus" because of its characteristic to connect all the computers in a straight line. If we through networking terms then this particular bus topology is considered to be the simplest and most common criteria to form any connection. The connecting cable among these devices is referred as trunk. In a bus the communication takes place because of three things which are discussed below: Sending a particular signal Bouncing of that signal Terminating the signal When a particular

16

signal is sent in terms of electronic signals, it carries the respective receiver computer address (I.P. address).The signal is sent to all the computers connected on the common, shared cable but only that device accepts whose address matches with the encoded signal address. This is good criteria of sending a signal but at the same time brings in a huge disadvantage of sending a signal by only one computer at a time. (Andrewferrier.com, 2017)This way if any computer have large data and is in process then others computer have to wait for a longer period of time.Somtime it may lead to process to die which is a serious issue. If the sent signal is left uninterrupted then it goes bouncing back and forth .This is a serious issue because this will not allow the cable to get free and thus other computers will not be able to send any sort of signal. Therefore, it is must to stop the signal once it has reached to its exact located device. This increases the efficiency of transmitting the data. Terminating the bouncing signal is done by the device named as terminator. It is located at the very end of each device and thus keeps terminating the bouncing signal. But the main issue with this topology is that, if anyhow one of the devices stops working then the whole system will be down. (Edrawsoft.com, 2017)Same is the case if the cable is unplugged at any end then it will put down the whole system. These needs to be taken care of while using the bus topology

The following sections contain both the advantages and disadvantages of using a bus topology with your devices.

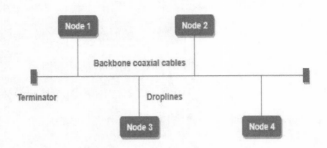

Figure 3 : A bus topology with shared backbone cable. The nodes are connected to the channel via drop lines.

Advantages of bus topology

- It works well when you have a small network.
- It's the easiest network topology for connecting computers or peripherals in a linear fashion.
- It requires less cable length than a star topology.

Disadvantages of bus topology

- It can be difficult to identify the problems if the whole network goes down.
- It can be hard to troubleshoot individual device issues.

- Bus topology is not great for large networks.

- Terminators are required for both ends of the main cable.

- Additional devices slow the network down.

If a main cable is damaged, the network fails or splits into two

Ring Topology

In the past, the ring topology was most commonly used in schools, offices, and smaller buildings where networks were smaller. However, today, the ring topology is seldom used, having been switched to another type of network topology for improved performance, stability, or support.

A ring topology is a network configuration in which device connections create a circular data path. Each networked device is connected to two others, like points on a circle. Together, devices in a ring topology are referred to as a ring network.

In a ring network, packets of data travel from one device to the next until they reach their destination. Most ring topologies allow packets to travel only in one direction, called a unidirectional ring network. Others permit data to move in either direction, called bidirectional.

The major disadvantage of a ring topology is that if any individual connection in the ring is broken, the entire network is affected.

Ring topologies may be used in either LANs (local area networks) or WANs (wide area networks). Depending on the type of network card used in each computer of the ring topology, a coaxial cable or an RJ-45 network cable is used to connect computers together.

Features of Ring Topology

A number of repeaters are used for Ring topology with large number of nodes, because if someone wants to send some data to the last node in the ring topology with 100 nodes, then the data will have to pass through 99 nodes to reach the 100th node. Hence to prevent data loss repeaters are used in the network. The transmission is unidirectional, but it can be made bidirectional by having 2 connections between each Network Node, it is called Dual Ring Topology. In Dual Ring Topology, two ring networks are formed, and data flow is in opposite direction in them. Also, if one ring fails, the second ring can act as a backup, to keep the network up. Data is transferred in a sequential manner that is bit by bit. Data transmitted, has to pass through each node of the network, till the destination node.

In this topology, it forms a ring connecting a devices with its exactly two neighbouring devices.

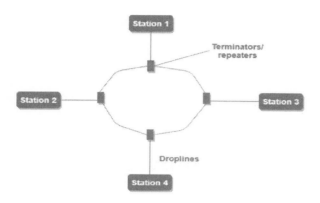

Figure 4 : A ring topology comprises of 4 stations connected with each forming a ring..

The following operations takes place in ring topology are :

1. One station is known as monitor station which takes all the responsibility to perform the operations.
2. To transmit the data, station has to hold the token. After the transmission is done, the token is to be released for other stations to use.
3. When no station is transmitting the data, then the token will circulate in the ring.

4. There are two types of token release techniques : Early token release releases the token just after the transmitting the data and Delay token release releases the token after the acknowledgement is received from the receiver.

Advantages of ring topology

- All data flows in one direction, reducing the chance of packet collisions.
- A network server is not needed to control network connectivity between each workstation.
- Data can transfer between workstations at high speeds.
- Additional workstations can be added without impacting performance of the network.

Disadvantages of ring topology

- All data being transferred over the network must pass through each workstation on the network, which can make it slower than a star topology.
- The entire network will be impacted if one workstation shuts down.

- The hardware needed to connect each workstation to the network is more expensive than Ethernet cards and hubs/switches.

The Hybrid Network Topology

The hybrid network topology includes a mix of bus topology, mesh topology, ring topology, star topology, and tree topology. The combination of topologies depends on the need of a company.

For example, if there is a Mesh topology in one office department while a Ring topology in another department, connecting these two with bus topology will result in Hybrid topology. Combination of Star-Ring and Star-Bus networks are the most common examples of the hybrid network topology.

Features of Bus Topology

1. It transmits data only in one direction.
2. Every device is connected to a single cable

This topology is a collection of two or more topologies which are described above. This is a scalable topology which can be expanded easily. It is reliable one but at the same it is a costly topology.

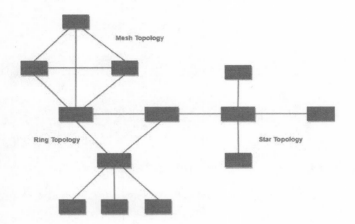

Figure 5 : A hybrid topology which is a combination of ring and star topology.

Advantages of Hybrid Topology:

1. Hybrid network combines the benefits of different types of topologies
2. Can be modified as per requirement
3. It is extremely flexible.
4. It is very reliable.
5. It is easily scalable

Disadvantages of Hybrid Topology:

1. It is expensive
2. The design of a hybrid network is complex.
3. Hardware changes are required in order to connect topology to another topology.

Tree Topology

In computer networks, a tree topology is also known as a star bus topology. It incorporates elements of both a bus topology and a star topology. Below is an example network diagram of a tree topology, in which the central nodes of two star networks are connected to one another. In the picture above, if the main cable or trunk between each of the two star topology networks were to fail, those networks would be unable to communicate with each other. However, computers on the same star topology would still be able to communicate.

A tree topology is a special type of structure in which many connected elements are arranged like the branches of a tree. For example, tree topologies are frequently used to organize the computers in a corporate network, or the information in a database.

In a tree topology, there can be only one connection between any two connected nodes. Because any two nodes can have only one mutual connection, tree topologies create a natural parent and child hierarchy.

Characteristics of Tree Topology

- Ideal if nodes are located in groups.
- Used in Wide Area Network.
- Better Flexibility
- Better Scalability

Tree topology in computer networking

In computer networks, a tree topology is also known as a star bus topology. It incorporates elements of both a bus topology and a star topology. Below is an example network diagram of a tree topology, in which the central nodes of two star networks are connected to one another.

Tree Topology

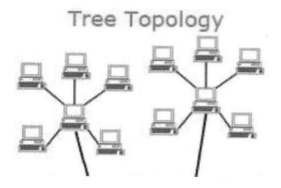

In the picture above, if the main cable or trunk between each of the two star topology networks were to fail, those networks would be unable to communicate with each other. However, computers on the same star topology would still be able to communicate.

Tree topology in computer programming

In computer programming, tree topologies can be used to structure many kinds of data, including a computer program itself.

For example, this is a computer program written in Lisp:

(+ 1 2 (if (> p 10) 3 4))

This program says "If p is greater than 10, add the numbers 1, 2, and 3. Otherwise, add the numbers 1, 2, and 4." Like all Lisp programs, it has an inherent tree topology structure. If we draw it as a graph, it looks like the tree shown at right. Representing a program this way can be useful because it clearly shows how all the operations and data are connected.

Programs in this kind of structure also have special uses. For instance, genetic programming techniques can evolve new computer programs by exchanging branches between existing programs structured as trees.

Tree topology in binary trees

A binary tree is a tree topology in which every node has a maximum of two children. The child nodes are labeled as "left child" or "right child." This type of data structure is often used for sorting and searching large amounts of data. In the binary tree shown below, each parent's left child has a value less than the right child.

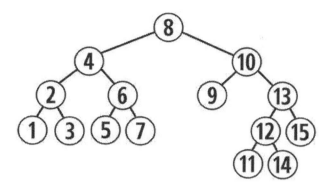

B-trees

A B-tree is a variation of a binary tree that was invented by Rudolf Bayer and Ed McCreight at Boeing Labs in 1971. Its nodes have children that fall within a predefined minimum and maximum, usually between 2 and 7. A B-tree graph might look like the image below.

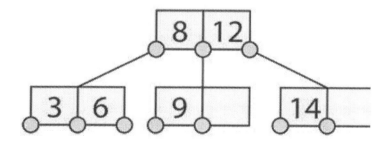

B-trees are "self-balancing," meaning the height of the branches is managed so that they do not get arbitrarily large. Each node contains partitioning "key values" that indicate the values of the children. Their design is optimized for handling very large data files, and for writing data to memory or disk. They are used extensively in database systems like MySQL, PostgreSQL, and Redis, and filesystems such as NTFS, HFS+, and ext4.

Advantages of Tree Topology

1. It is a combination of bus and star topology
2. It provides high scalability, as leaf nodes can add more nodes in the hierarchical chain.
3. Other nodes in a network are not affected, if one of their nodes get damaged
4. It provides easy maintenance and fault identification.
5. Supported by several hardware and software vendors.
6. Point-to-point wiring for individual segments.

Disadvantages of Tree Topology

1. Large cabling is required as compared to star and bus topology.
2. On the failure of a hub, the entire network fails.

Tree network is very difficult to configure than other network topologies

TRANSMISSION MODES IN COMPUTER NETWORKS

Transmission mode refers to the mechanism of transferring of data between two devices connected over a network. It is also called Communication Mode. These modes direct the direction of flow of information. There are three types of transmission modes. They are:

1. Simplex Mode
2. Half duplex Mode
3. Full duplex Mode

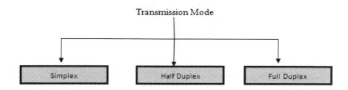

Simplex Mode

In this type of transmission mode, data can be sent only in one direction i.e. communication is unidirectional. We cannot send a message back to the sender. Unidirectional communication is done in Simplex Systems where we just need to send a command/signal, and do not expect any response back.

Examples of simplex Mode are loudspeakers, television broadcasting, television and remote, keyboard and monitor etc.

Half Duplex Mode

Half-duplex data transmission means that data can be transmitted in both directions on a signal carrier, but not at the same time.

For example, on a local area network using a technology that has half-duplex transmission, one workstation can send data on the line and then immediately receive data on the line from the same direction in which data was just transmitted. Hence half-duplex transmission implies a bidirectional line (one that can carry data in both directions) but data can be sent in only one direction at a time.

Example of half duplex is a walkie- talkie in which message is sent one at a time but messages are sent in both the directions.

Full Duplex Mode

In full duplex system we can send data in both the directions as it is bidirectional at the same time in other words, data can be sent in both directions simultaneously.

Example of Full Duplex is a Telephone Network in which there is communication between two persons by a telephone line, using which both can talk and listen at the same time.

In full duplex system there can be two lines one for sending the data and the other for receiving data.

Transmission Mediums in Computer Networks

Transmission Mediums in Computer Networks are the physical pathways that connect computers, and other devices on a network.Each transmission medium requires specialized network hardware that has to be compatible with that medium.

33

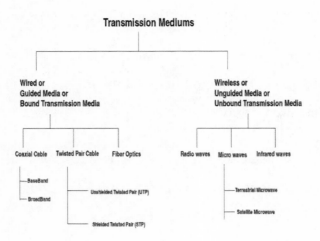

Transmission Mediums in Computer Networks is broadly classified into two groups.

Wired or Guided Media or Bound Transmission Media :

A signal travelling along any of these media is directed and contained by the physical limits of the medium.Popular bound transmission media in use are twisted pair cable, co-axial cable and fiber optical cable.It can be classified depending its own characteristics that is cost, transmission speed, physical appearance etc.

Wireless or Unguided Media or Unbound Transmission Media

Wireless or unguided media are communicate using electromagnetic waves. Its very popular now.It use Microwave, Radio wave, Infra red for communication with out physical medium.

Some of Factors to be consider in Data Transmission

1. Bandwidth : It refers to the data carrying capacity higher the bandwidth will be higher the data transfer rate.
2. Radiation : It refers to the leakage of signal from the medium.
3. Noise reduction : noise is an error in information signal. Hence noise must be remove from the signal this process is called as noise   reduction.
4. Attenuation : It refers to loss of energy in a signal transmission.

Twisted Pair Cable

A twisted pair cable helps to reduce crosstalk and electromagnetic induction this is because it is made of two twisted copper wires twisted . Out of these two wires, only one carries actual signal and another is used for ground reference.

Some important points :

Its frequency range is 0 to 3.5 kHz.

Typical attenuation is 0.2 dB/Km @ 1kHz.

Typical delay is 50 µs/km.

Repeater spacing is 2km.

Twisted Pair is of two types:

Unshielded Twisted Pair (UTP) s

Shielded Twisted Pair (STP)

STP cables comes with twisted wire pair covered in metal foil. This makes it more indifferent to noise and crosstalk.

UTP cables has seven categories, each suitable for specific use. In computer networks, Cat-5, Cat-5e, and Cat-6 cables are mostly used. UTP cables are connected by RJ45 connectors.

Cable Type	Speed
CAT 3	16Mbps
CAT 5	100Mbps 1000Mbps (4 pairs)
CAT 5E	1000Mbps
CAT 6	Up to 400MHz for super-fast Broadbandapplications

Coaxial Cable

Coaxial cable has two wires of copper. The core wire lies in the center and it is made of solid conductor.The core is enclosed in an insulating sheath.The second wire is wrapped around over the sheath and that too in turn encased by insulator sheath.This all is covered by plastic cover. Here the most common coaxial standards.

50-Ohm RG-7 or RG-11 used with thick Ethernet

50-Ohm RG-58   used with thin Ethernet

75-Ohm RG-59   used with cable television

93-Ohm RG-62   used with ARCNET

Each cable defined by an RG rating is adapted for a specialized function, as shown in the table below:

The below figure shows 3 popular types of these connectors: the BNC Connector, the BNC T connector and the BNC terminator.

The BNC connector is used to connect the end of the cable to the device, such as a TV set. The BNC T connector is used in Ethernet networks to branch out to a connection to a computer or other device. The BNC terminator is used at the end of the cable to prevent the reflection of the signal.

There are two types of Coaxial cables :

1. BaseBand

This is a 50 ohm (Ω) coaxial cable which is used for digital transmission. It is mostly used for LAN's. Baseband transmits a single signal at a time with very high speed. The major drawback is that it needs amplification after every 1000 feet.

2. BroadBand

This uses analog transmission on standard cable television cabling. It transmits several simultaneous signal using different frequencies. It covers large area when compared with Baseband Coaxial Cable.

Bandwidth is high

Used in long distance telephone lines.

Transmits digital signals at a very high rate of 10Mbps.

Coaxial cable was widely used in analog telephone networks, where a single coaxial network could carry 10,000 voice signals. Cable TV networks also use coaxial cables. In the traditional cable

TV network, the entire network used coaxial cable. Cable TV uses RG-59 coaxial cable.

Fiber Optics or Optical Fiber

Signal is transmitted by use of light through the glass fiber.From one end of it light is emitted, it travels through it and at the other end light detector detects light stream and converts it to electric data. It provides an electrical isolation and totally reduces electromagnetic interference or noise by surrounding equipment. installing and connecting the fibers requires special equipment. The transmission rate can exceed 2 G bps, nowdays around 6 ~8G bps and is the highest transmission medium in the world. Fiber Optic provides the highest mode of speed. It comes in two modes, one is single mode fiber and second is multimode fiber. Single mode fiber can carry a single ray of light whereas multimode is capable of carrying multiple beams of light.

The below figure shows how a ray of light changes direction when going from a more dense to a less dense substance.

Internal view of an Optical fibre

UnBounded or UnGuided Transmission Media

Unguided medium transport electromagnetic waves without using a physical conductor. This type of communication is often referred to as wireless communication. Signals are normally broadcast through free space and thus are available to anyone who has a device   capable   of   receiving   them. The below figure shows the part of the electromagnetic spectrum, ranging from 3 kHz to 900 THz, used for wireless communication.

Unguided signals can travel from the source to the destination in several ways: Gound propagation, Sky propagation and Line-of-sight propagation as shown in below figure.

Propagation Modes

Ground Propagation : In this, radio waves travel through the lowest portion of the atmosphere, hugging the Earth. These low-frequency signals emanate in all directions from the transmitting antenna   and   follow   the   curvature   of   the   planet. Sky Propagation : In this, higher-frequency radio waves radiate upward into the ionosphere where they are reflected back to Earth. This type of transmission allows for greater distances with lower   output   power. Line-of-sight Propagation : in this type, very high-frequency signals are transmitted in straight lines directly from antenna to antenna.

We can divide wireless transmission into three broad groups:
1. Radio waves
2. Micro waves
3. Infrared waves

Radio Waves

Electromagnetic waves ranging in frequencies between 3 KHz and 1 GHz are normally called radio waves
Radio waves are omnidirectional. When an antenna transmits radio waves, they are propagated in all directions. The omnidirectional property has disadvantage, too. The radio waves transmitted by one antenna are susceptible to interference by another antenna that may send signal suing the same frequency or band.
Radio waves, particularly with those of low and medium frequencies, can penetrate walls. It is an advantage because, an AM radio can receive signals inside a building. It is a disadvantage because we cannot isolate a communication to just inside or outside a building.

Omnidirectional Antenna for Radio Waves

Radio waves use omnidirectional antennas that send out signals in all directions.

Applications of Radio Waves

The omnidirectional characteristics of radio waves make them useful for multicasting in which there is one sender but many receivers.

AM and FM radio, television, maritime radio, cordless phones, and paging are examples of multicasting.

Micro Waves

Microwave relays

It consists of transmission tower responsible for transmitting or repeating the signal for each hop. Electromagnetic waves having frequencies between 1 and 300 GHz are called micro waves. Micro waves are unidirectional .The distance is around 30 Kilometers to 50 Kilometers. The transmission rate can be up to 250M bps. The transmission quality however is subject to weather changes. The use of microwave is ideal for short-haul and high bandwidth applications due to no cabling cost once the transmission tower is built.

Microwaves are very useful when unicast(one-to-one) communication is needed between the sender and the receiver. They are used in cellular phones, satellite networks and wireless LANs.

There are 2 types of Microwave Transmission :

1. Terrestrial Microwave

2. Satellite Microwave

Terrestrial Microwave

Terrestrial microwave use repeaters with antenna for increasing the signal distance .The signal received by an antenna can be converted into transmittable form and relayed to next antenna. It is an example of telephone systems all over the world

Parabolic Antenna

A parabolic reflector, dish, or mirror is a device that is used to collect or project energy such as electromagnetic waves. Alter incoming plane waves traveling along the same axis as the parabola into a wave that is spherical and they all meet at the focus of the reflector.

The parabolic dish antenna is the form most frequently used in the radar engineering of installed antenna types of. Figure 1 illustrates the parabolic antenna. A dish antenna consists of one circular parabolic reflector and a point source situated in the focal point of this reflector. This point source is called "primary feed" or "feed".

The circular parabolic (paraboloid) reflector is constructed of metal, usually, a frame covered by metal mesh at the inner side. The width of the slots of the metal mesh has to be less than $\lambda/10$. This metal covering forms the reflector acting as a mirror for the radar energy.

According to the laws of optics and analytical geometry, for this type of reflector all reflected rays will be parallel to the axis of the paraboloid which gives us ideally one single reflected ray parallel to the main axis with no sidelobes. The field leaves this feed horn with a spherical wavefront. As each part of the wavefront reaches the reflecting surface, it is shifted 180 degrees in phase and sent outward at angles that cause all parts of the field to travel in parallel paths.

This is an idealized radar antenna and produces a pencil beam. If the reflector has an elliptical shape, then it will produce a fan beam. Surveillance radars use two different curvatures in the horizontal and vertical planes to achieve the required pencil beam in azimuth and the classical cosecant squared fan beam in elevation.

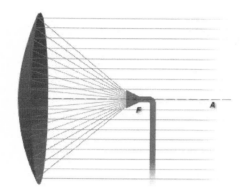

Horn antennas are very popular at UHF (300 MHz-3 GHz) and higher frequencies (I've heard of horn antennas operating as high as 140 GHz). Horn antennas often have a directional radiation pattern with a high antenna gain, which can range up to 25 dB in some cases, with 10-20 dB being typical. Horn antennas have a wide impedance bandwidth, implying that the input impedance is slowly varying over a wide frequency range (which also implies low values for S11 or VSWR). The bandwidth for practical horn antennas can be on the order of 20:1 (for instance, operating from 1 GHz-20 GHz), with a 10:1 bandwidth not being uncommon.

The gain of horn antennas often increases (and the beamwidth decreases) as the frequency of operation is increased. This is because the size of the horn aperture is always measured in wavelengths; at higher frequencies the horn antenna is "electrically larger"; this is because a higher frequency has a smaller wavelength. Since the horn antenna has a fixed physical size (say a square aperture of 20 cm across, for instance), the aperture is more wavelengths across at higher frequencies. And, a recurring theme in antenna theory is that larger antennas (in terms of wavelengths in size) have higher directivities.

Horn antennas have very little loss, so the directivity of a horn is roughly equal to its gain.

Horn antennas are somewhat intuitive and relatively simple to manufacture. In addition, acoustic horn antennas are also used in transmitting sound waves (for example, with a megaphone). Horn antennas are also often used to feed a dish antenna, or as a "standard gain" antenna in measurements.

Popular versions of the horn antenna include the E-plane horn, shown in Figure 1. This horn antenna is flared in the E-plane, giving the name. The horizontal dimension is constant at w.

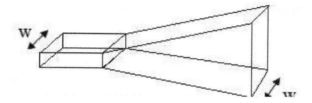

Figure 1. E-plane horn antenna.

Another example of a horn antenna is the H-plane horn, shown in Figure 2. This horn is flared in the H-plane, with a constant height for the waveguide and horn of h.

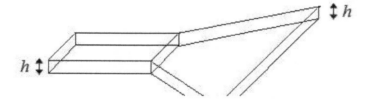

Figure 2. H-Plane horn antenna.

The most popular horn antenna is flared in both planes as shown in Figure 3. This is a pyramidal horn, and has a width B and height A at the end of the horn.

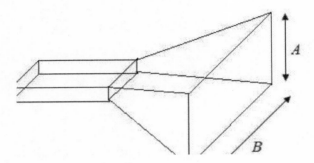

Figure 3. Pyramidal horn antenna.

Horn antennas are typically fed by a section of a waveguide, as shown in Figure 4. The waveguide itself is often fed with a short dipole, which is shown in red in Figure 4. A waveguide is simply a hollow, metal cavity (see the waveguide tutorial). Waveguides are used to guide electromagnetic energy from one place to another. The waveguide in Figure 4 is a rectangular waveguide of width b and height a, with b>a. The E-field distribution for the dominant mode is shown in the lower part of Figure 1.

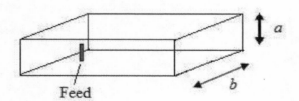

Feed

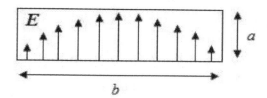

Figure 4. Waveguide used as a feed to horn antennas.

Fields and Geometrical Parameters for Horn Antennas

Antenna texts typically derive very complicated functions for the radiation patterns of horn antennas. To do this, first the E-field across the aperture of the horn antenna is assumed to be known, and the far-field radiation pattern is calculated using the radiation equations. While this is conceptually straight forward, the resulting field functions end up being extremely complex, and personally I don't feel add a whole lot of value. If you would like to see these derivations, pick up any antenna textbook that has a section on horn antennas. (Also, as a practicing antenna engineer, I can assure you that we never use radiation integrals to estimate patterns. We always go on previous experience, computer simulations and measurements.)

Instead of the traditional academic derivation approach, I'll state some results for the horn antenna and show some typical radiation patterns, and attempt to provide a feel for the design parameters of horn antennas. Since the pyramidal horn antenna is the most popular, we'll analyze that. The E-field distribution across the aperture of the horn antenna is what is responsible for the radiation.

The radiation pattern of a horn antenna will depend on B and A (the dimensions of the horn at the opening) and R (the length of the horn, which also affects the flare angles of the horn), along with b and a (the dimensions of the waveguide).

Satellite Microwave

This is a microwave relay station which is placed in outer space. Signal is transmitted up and down between ground stations. The satellite is therefore used as a repeater for re-generating the signal.

These are positioned 36000 Km above the equator with an orbit speed that exactly matches the rotation speed of the earth. This is usually done to allow ground stations to aim antenna at a fixed point in the sky. Satellite manufacturing cost is very high

.Transmission highly depends on whether conditions, it can go down in bad weather

Advantages of Satellite Communication

Here are the list of some main advantages of satellite communication:

- The area coverage through the satellite transmission is large
- The heavy usage of intercontinental traffic makes the satellite commercial attractive
- Satellites can cover large areas of the Earth. This is particularly useful for sparsely populated areas

Disadvantages of Satellite Communication

Here are the list of some main disadvantages of satellite communication:

- Technological limitations preventing the deployment of large, high gain antennas on the satellite platform
- Over-crowding of available bandwidths due to low antenna gains

- The high investment cost of insurance cost associated with significant probability of failure
- High atmospheric losses above 30 GHz limit carrier frequencies

Infrared Waves

Infrared waves, with frequencies from 300 GHz to 400 THz, can be used for short-range communication. Infrared waves, with high frequencies, cannot penetrate walls. This prevents interference between one system and with another system.

It is a region of the electromagnetic radiation spectrum where wavelengths range from about 700 nanometers (nm) to 1 millimeter (mm). Infrared waves are longer than those of visible light, but shorter than those of radio waves.

Remote controls use near-infrared light, transmitted with light-emitting diodes (LEDs), to send focused signals to home-entertainment devices, such as televisions. Infrared light is also used in fiber optic cables to transmit data.

Infrared radiation (IR), or infrared light, is a type of radiant energy that's invisible to human eyes but that we can feel as heat. All objects in the universe emit some level of IR radiation, but two of the most obvious sources are the sun and fire.

IR is a type of electromagnetic radiation, a continuum of frequencies produced when atoms absorb and then release energy. From highest to lowest frequency, electromagnetic radiation includes gamma-rays, X-rays, ultraviolet radiation, visible light, infrared radiation, microwaves and radio waves. Together, these types of radiation make up the electromagnetic spectrum.

British astronomer William Herschel discovered infrared light in 1800, according to NASA. In an experiment to measure the difference in temperature between the colors in the visible spectrum, he placed thermometers in the path of light within each color of the visible spectrum. He observed an increase in temperature from blue to red, and he found an even warmer temperature measurement just beyond the red end of the visible spectrum.

Within the electromagnetic spectrum, infrared waves occur at frequencies above those of microwaves and just below those of red visible light, hence the name "infrared." Waves of infrared radiation are longer than those of visible light, according to the California Institute of Technology (Caltech). IR frequencies range from about 3 gigahertz (GHz) up to about 400 terahertz (THz), and wavelengths are estimated to range between 1,000 micrometers (μm) and 760 nanometers (2.9921 inches), although these values are not definitive, according to NASA.

Similar to the visible light spectrum, which ranges from violet (the shortest visible-light wavelength) to red (longest wavelength), infrared radiation has its own range of wavelengths. The shorter "near-infrared" waves, which are closer to visible light on the electromagnetic spectrum, don't emit any detectable heat and are what's discharged from a TV remote control to change the channels. The longer "far-infrared" waves, which are closer to the microwave section on the electromagnetic spectrum, can be felt as intense heat, such as the heat from sunlight or fire, according to NASA.

IR radiation is one of the three ways heat is transferred from one place to another, the other two being convection and conduction. Everything with a temperature above around 5 degrees Kelvin (minus 450 degrees Fahrenheit or minus 268 degrees Celsius) emits IR radiation. The sun gives off half of its total energy as IR, and much of the star's visible light is absorbed and re-emitted as IR, according to the University of Tennessee.

Household uses

Household appliances such as heat lamps and toasters use IR radiation to transmit heat, as do industrial heaters such as those used for drying and curing materials. Incandescent bulbs convert only about 10 percent of their electrical energy input into visible light energy, while the other 90 percent is converted to infrared radiation, according to the Environmental Protection Agency.

Infrared lasers can be used for point-to-point communications over distances of a few hundred meters or yards. TV remote controls that rely on infrared radiation shoot out pulses of IR energy from a light-emitting diode (LED) to an IR receiver in the TV, according to How Stuff Works. The receiver converts the light pulses to electrical signals that instruct a microprocessor to carry out the programmed command.

Infrared sensing

One of the most useful applications of the IR spectrum is in sensing and detection. All objects on Earth emit IR radiation in the form of heat. This can be detected by electronic sensors, such as those used in night vision goggles and infrared cameras.

A simple example of such a sensor is the bolometer, which consists of a telescope with a temperature-sensitive resistor, or thermistor, at its focal point, according to the University of California, Berkeley (UCB). If a warm body comes into this instrument's field of view, the heat causes a detectable change in the voltage across the thermistor.

Night vision cameras use a more sophisticated version of a bolometer. These cameras typically contain charge-coupled device (CCD) imaging chips that are sensitive to IR light. The image formed by the CCD can then be reproduced in visible light. These systems can be made small enough to be used in hand-held devices or wearable night-vision goggles. The cameras can also be used for gun sights with or without the addition of an IR laser for targeting.

Infrared spectroscopy measures IR emissions from materials at specific wavelengths. The IR spectrum of a substance will show characteristic dips and peaks as photons (particles of light) are absorbed or emitted by electrons in molecules as the electrons transition between orbits, or energy levels. This spectroscopic information can then be used to identify substances and monitor chemical reactions.

According to Robert Mayanovic, professor of physics at Missouri State University, infrared spectroscopy, such as Fourier transform infrared (FTIR) spectroscopy, is highly useful for numerous scientific applications. These include the study of molecular systems and 2D materials, such as graphene.

Infrared astronomy

Caltech describes infrared astronomy as "the detection and study of the infrared radiation (heat energy) emitted from objects in the universe." Advances in IR CCD imaging systems have allowed for detailed observation of the distribution of IR sources in space, revealing complex structures in nebulas, galaxies and the large-scale structure of the universe.

One of the advantages of IR observation is that it can detect objects that are too cool to emit visible light. This has led to the discovery of previously unknown objects, including comets, asteroids and wispy interstellar dust clouds that seem to be prevalent throughout the galaxy.

IR astronomy is particularly useful for observing cold molecules of gas and for determining the chemical makeup of dust particles in the interstellar medium, said Robert Patterson, professor of astronomy at Missouri State University. These observations are conducted using specialized CCD detectors that are sensitive to IR photons.

Another advantage of IR radiation is that its longer wavelength means it doesn't scatter as much as visible light, according to NASA. Whereas visible light can be absorbed or reflected by gas and dust particles, the longer IR waves simply go around these small obstructions. Because of this property, IR can be used to observe objects whose light is obscured by gas and dust. Such objects include newly forming stars imbedded in nebulas or the center of Earth's galaxy.

ONCLUSION

he conclusion of network topology is to ensure that the system is working as required. Topology refers to the physical wiring process in a network.

Made in the USA
Las Vegas, NV
07 January 2022

40768204R00035